FOUNDATION
FOR AN EFFECTIVE
YOUTH MINISTRY

5

Point Thrust for Success

Lawanne' S. Grant, Ph.D.

FOUNDATION
FOR AN EFFECTIVE
YOUTH MINISTRY

5

Point Thrust for Success

Lawanne' S. Grant, Ph.D.

NUVISION PUBLISHING

Editor: Nancy Arant Williams
Cover Design: Darryl Chandler

Scripture taken from The Holy Bible, KJV 1769 edition, public domain.

Scripture quotation marked NLT are taken from the Holy Bible, New Living Translation, copyright, 1996, 2004, 2007, by Tyndale House Foundation. Used by permission of Tyndale House Publishers, Inc. Carol Stream, Illinois, 60188. All rights reserved.

Books may be ordered through booksellers or by contacting:

Leadership DevelopME, LLC
P.O. Box 481048
Charlotte, NC 28269
www.leadershipdevelopme.com
(704) 659-3882

ISBN 978-0-578-19006-8

NVP
NUVISION PUBLISHING
PO Box 4455 | Wilmington NC
www.nuvisiondesigns.biz

Printed in the United States of America.

CONTENTS

Acknowledgements 7

Introduction...9

Chapter 1   Energetic Leaders 15

                What is a Youth Leader? 15

                What are necessary characteristics
of a Youth Leader? 15

                How do I identify effective Youth
Leaders? 17

                How do I organize my team of Youth
Leaders? 18

                Job Descriptions 19

                Are you an energetic leader?.............22

Chapter 2   Evangelism 25

                What is evangelism as it relates to
youth? 25

                How can I effectively witness to youth?....26

Chapter 3   Educational Development...................35

                What is education and why is it
important? 35

                How do I educate youth naturally?......36

                How can I make certain that the youth
are spiritually equipped for life? 40

What are other methods of promoting education? 43

Chapter 4   Active Auxiliaries 47

Why are active auxiliaries vital to a youth department? 47

Description of Auxiliaries....................50

Chapter 5   Annual Affairs 57

What type of annual affairs should my youth department host? 57

Chapter 6   Write it & Make it Happen...................65

Chapter 7   Conclusion 73

ACKNOWLEDGEMENTS

This book is dedicated to the youth of this generation and generations to come. For as long as I can remember, I've been involved in youth ministry either as a youth or a youth leader, working in the community, academic setting, work environment, and church auxiliaries. My heart's desire is to equip youth leaders to minister to the very best of their ability.

I am extremely honored and grateful that God would give me such passion for youth and youth leaders. Everything I am and have to offer is because of Him. *For God is working in you, giving you the desire and the power to do what pleases him (Phil. 2:13, NLT).*

As with every project, business endeavor, and personal accomplishment, I'd like to thank my family and friends for always pushing me forward! Last, but definitely not least, I want to say **thank you** to my husband Darryl L. Grant, for always listening to my preliminary thoughts, ideas, and strategies.

Now that you're familiar with the important people in my life, let's dive in to make sure your youth ministry has a powerful and effective foundation.

INTRODUCTION

...Behold, I lay in Zion for a foundation a stone, a tried stone, a precious stone, a sure foundation... (Isaiah 28:16).

Have you ever been a part of or been familiar with an organization that appeared to be at the top of its game? To the casual observer, everything appeared robust, earning the accolades due a successful, thriving organization. Then you were shocked to discover that wasn't true only when the bottom fell out to expose previously unknown cracks in its foundation. Further investigation revealed that either its policies and practices were at fault or a key player began playing by rules that would be to his own advantage rather than protecting company interests. Your initial response was probably: they could've avoided such a catastrophic fall had they done things by the book.

Guess what, you're absolutely right! It's absurd to imagine that any company would include failure in its projected business plan. Its mission statement/goals alone would confirm its intentions to flourish. In fact, unless we constantly check the plumb line to see if we're still on the straight and narrow toward healthy, measurable goals, with no deviation in direction, we too could find ourselves on shaky ground.

This is particularly important with regard to the body of Christ—His church. Youth of various backgrounds confront and seek answers for messy, uncomfortable, embarrassing and awkward issues, even life-threatening situations. In fact, they don't have to look very far to find a wide variety of options that seem to address them, but the question is: do those options line up with true foundational Christian principles that have proved effective in the past? That should be the one and only standard we use, as we seek to inspire our youth to follow the path of wisdom. If that's our goal, we will not fail to create a powerful outreach that will impact our precious youth for generations to come.

This process is by no means exhaustive, but uses a five-point thrust--a solid base of checks and balances to keep us on track regardless of the size of the organization. The components of the five-point thrust are:

- ➢ Energetic Leaders
- ➢ Evangelism
- ➢ Educational Development

- ➢ Active Auxiliaries
- ➢ Annual Affairs

The Lord spoke to Habakkuk and instructed him, "…write the vision and make it plain…" (Habakkuk 2:2). The five-point thrust will assist you as you write **your** vision and make it plain for all to follow that they may mature spiritually and naturally to live out their God-given destiny.

5-POINT THRUST

Energetic Leaders

Evangelism

Educational Development

Active Auxiliaries

Annual Affairs

Triple E + Double A =
Successful Youth of Today

Youth Leaders' Discussion Forum

1. Why is it important to base your youth ministry on solid foundational principles?

2. What are the pros and cons of using a checks and balance system to measure your current practices?

3. Considering what you know so far about the 5-point thrust, which component would you argue is the most important? Why?

Chapter 1

ENERGETIC LEADERS

Even them will I bring to my holy mountain, and make them joyful in my house of prayer... (Isaiah 56:7).

What is a Youth Leader?

Youth leaders are gifted with the ability to inspire and supervise the youth in discovering both known and unknown gifts and talents. They are also aware of outside influences that can impact the lives of youth, either for good or for harm. Additionally, they are skilled in guiding youth toward sound wisdom that will stabilize their here and now, and guard their future.

What are necessary characteristics of a Youth Leader?

Approachable	Excited
Available	Energetic
Committed	Knowledgeable
Consistent	Organized

Creative	Patient
Dedicated	Prayerful
Determined	Sensitive
Disciplined	Trustworthy
Enthused	Wise

During your own childhood, you were probably able to identify those who truly cared about youth. This enabled you to discern the difference between those who were fakes and those you could trust when you had a serious problem that demanded true wisdom.

We live in a time that can be very risky for youth. With a wide range of choices so very accessible, it's easy to fall victim to foolish schemes without the input of a healthy support system. Young people seek sources for real, practical wisdom, something that helps them cope and offers strength to overcome and endure, enabling them to stand up against the relentless pressures that bombard them on a daily basis. For that reason, it's vital that youth leaders move in love highly motivated to encourage and inspire youth with hope, urging them to diligently seek God for the ability to make wise and honorable decisions. If youth leaders are energetic, the youth will be inspired. That's why it's so important that leadership positions are filled with those who are passionate about those in their care. In fact, anyone who is not motivated, passionate, or energetic need not apply.

How do I identify effective Youth Leaders?

Unless you're seeking someone with specific qualifications or education, it's not necessary to force unwilling workers to sign up to work with youth. In reality, coerced individuals rarely if ever live up to a leader's hopeful expectations. If you are in a position to recruit workers, it helps to keep an eye out for those who already work within the ministry without the need for a formal position or title, because these individuals tend to be dedicated and productive workers.

It's vital to get a positive recommendation for anyone you're considering as a potential youth leader. It should come from a pastor or other primary leader within the church or ministry. It should either solidly confirm or disagree with your assessment regarding your candidate's leadership characteristics and qualities.

Once that issue is settled, you're ready to take the next step in the recruitment process. Remember that this candidate should possess most if not all the

Lawanne' S. Grant

qualities previously mentioned. To sum up, the following three steps will aid in the selection of the best person for the job—Identification, Recommendation, and finally Integration.

How do I organize my team of Youth Leaders?

If there is to be any hope of experiencing a true move of God within the group, the leadership must be in agreement, submitted within a prescribed structure. Apart from unity among the leaders, there will be strife that hinders, even prohibits an authentic experience with God. In order to be effectively unified in their leadership roles, leaders should understand the organizational structure and the expectations required.

Depending on the size of your organization, at least for a time, there will be a number of positions in which to serve, and some leaders may work in more than one capacity. In case of panic, consider this; in time, you'll have more than enough help as your warm and loving enthusiasm attracts others to your team. The following is an organizational chart of a standard youth department. Add or delete components of this subset to accommodate the needs of your ministry.

```
                    ┌──────────────┐
                    │    PASTOR    │
                    └──────┬───────┘
                 ┌─────────┴─────────┐
                 │  YOUTH DIRECTOR   │
                 └─────────┬─────────┘
            ┌──────────────┴──────────────┐
            │  ASSISTANT YOUTH DIRECTOR   │
            └──────────────┬──────────────┘
          ┌────────────────┴────────────────┐
          │   YOUTH/AUXILIARY LEADERS        │
          └──┬────────────────────────────┬──┘
   ┌─────────┴─────────────┐    ◄►    ┌────┴──────────────────┐
   │ ASSISTANT STAFF MEMBERS│         │  JUNIOR STAFF MEMBERS │
   └───────────┬────────────┘         └───────────────────────┘
              ┌┴──────────────────┐
              │ YOUTH AUXILIARIES │
              └───────────────────┘
```

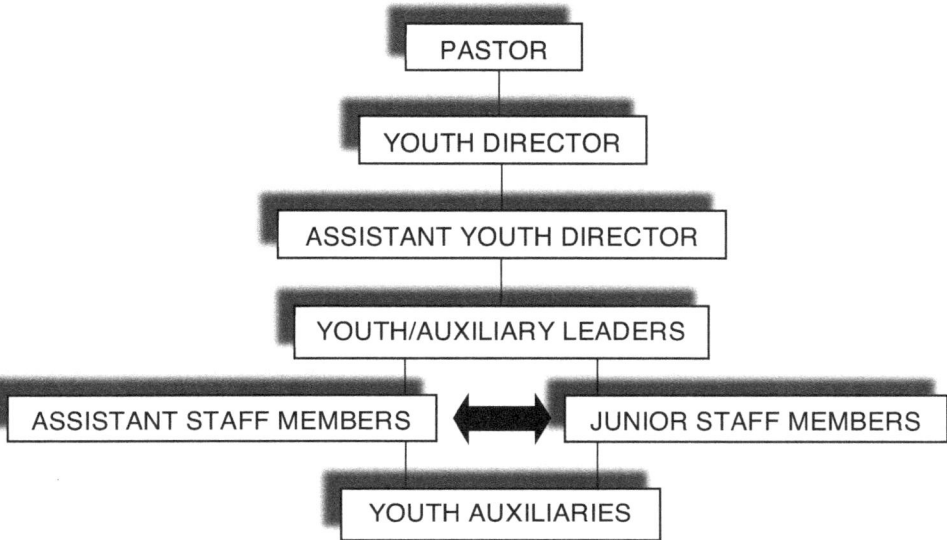

JOB DESCRIPTIONS:

PASTOR: Your pastor is the overseer and shepherd of the entire church family. The youth director generally receives his or her appointment and instructions from the pastor.

YOUTH DIRECTOR: The youth director, whose title is interchangeable with the term "youth pastor", oversees the entire scope of youth department activities. It's this person's responsibility to create a plan that is in sync with the pastor's vision for the youth department and reaching specified goals.

He/she is responsible for keeping the pastor informed of facts pertinent to the youth department. This person will also communicate and obtain approval for any planned youth activities and may also be put in charge of the department funds and their proper use. This will include establishing a team responsible for approving and tracking incoming and outgoing monies, as well as identifying and appointing capable youth leaders and volunteers who will powerfully impact the youth.

ASSISTANT YOUTH DIRECTOR: The assistant youth director works closely with, and under the supervision of the youth director. He or she is primarily responsible for ensuring that the vision of the youth director is fulfilled. This includes monitoring the operations of the various auxiliaries and remaining abreast of all department activities. This individual must be flexible, ready and available to stand in when the youth director is unavailable.

YOUTH/AUXILIARY LEADERS: Youth leaders are chosen, appointed by the pastor and youth director to be the primary moderators of a specific auxiliary. They are responsible for the operation and function of their assigned auxiliary. Ideally, youth leaders should spearhead only one auxiliary, but not be exempt from participation in others.

ASSISTANT STAFF MEMBERS: Assistant staff members are appointed by the youth/auxiliary leaders and work closely with them to fulfill the vision of the auxiliary. They must be readily available to assist at the request of the youth/auxiliary leader.

JUNIOR STAFF MEMBERS: Junior staff members shadow assistant staff members and help to carry out their duties. Ideally, these individuals are between the ages of twelve and eighteen but can be younger or older. Their input will provide youth leaders with the youth's invaluable perspective when planning and organizing events.

YOUTH AUXILIARIES: Youth auxiliaries are the nucleus of the youth department. They are designed to engage and encourage the involvement of young people, motivating them to exercise their talents and gifts as members of the drama team, sign language team, praise team, etc.

Are you an ENERGETIC leader?

E — Empathetic when needed

N — Never too busy to help in a crisis

E — Engages in youthful activities

R — Redirects negative behavior with love

G — Gathers facts to remain relevant in approach

E — Excited about accomplishments yet encouraging in the face of failure

T — Talks with authority but doesn't behave like an authoritarian

I — Interested in what's going on in the world of young people

C — Committed to the success of young people even when they aren't committed to themselves

Youth Leaders' Discussion Forum

1. Does everybody have the potential to be a youth leader? Why or Why not?

2. Identify 5 people who demonstrate passion and are already informally working with young people. What can they offer to your youth department? Discuss your plan to engage and formally integrate them into the operation of your youth department.

3. Why is it important to provide a written job description to leaders, volunteers, and others working within the youth department?

Chapter 2

EVANGELISM

...Go into the highway and the hedges, and compel them to come in, that my house may be filled (St. Luke 14:23).

What is evangelism as it relates to youth?

Evangelism is simply zealous preaching and teaching done to further the gospel of Jesus Christ. It serves as a venue to reach and make youth aware of their divine destiny. The act of evangelism often requires repetition in order to radically impact youth with the truth.

It's past time for traditional "revivals" in order to welcome the concept of true evangelism: empowering youth, to radically impact their daily lives. Too often we organize a youth event thinking we have accomplished the goal of evangelism, when it would have made far more of an impact to have the youth involved from the inception, in planning and prayer, believing God is going to move in response to their sincere petitions. This is the epitome of boots-on-the-ground training toward growth and godliness. Putting first things first, we must stop expecting an external harvest before we invest in the inner man, in order to produce an internal harvest. In other words, in-reach comes before outreach. The greatest moves of God spring from the hearts of transformed people who have no other agenda than passion for Christ and love for the lost. Such passion will inspire others to want that passion for themselves. For instance, the testimony of a young person radically delivered from drugs will have far greater impact than a lecture from someone who has not fought the same battles. To that end, we as leaders must equip our youth to be ready in season and out of season to share their stories with those who need to hear.

How can I effectively witness to youth?

In order to witness effectively we must be willing to customize our approach to evangelism, inviting the Holy Spirit to speak to that person's felt need. By that I mean we mustn't expect a one-size-fits-all message to speak to the young when they need to hear that it offers answers and wisdom found nowhere else, addressing tough issues like teen pregnancy, gang involvement, suicide, rejection, bullying and mental illness to name only a few.

There are multiple approaches to youth evangelism, but no matter which course you take, allow your youth to be involved in the decision-making process, motivating them to minister to the needs of others. Youth leaders and other adults should supervise the process, so that all things are done decently and in order. *(I Cor. 14:40)*

The size of your youth department will determine whether or not you will need the assistance of another organization to successfully carry out your vision. Perhaps you will need to partner with local organizations such as a sister church, community center, local school, etc. Be mindful that your outreach should be held in an area easily accessible to those you want to reach.

Highlighted below are only a few suggested outreach projects you might want to consider:

- Weekly/Monthly Youth Night Gatherings
- "Fun Night"
- Community Awareness Day
- Park Services

- Open Forums
- Juvenile Hall Outreach – "Behind Closed Doors"

YOUTH NIGHT GATHERINGS: Young people are always searching for a place to "hang out," particularly on the weekends. Set a specific predictable weekend day/date, and host a youth night service. Create an appealing name for the gathering. Instead of calling it youth night, why not call it "Friday Night Live" or "The SPOT"? If you selected "The SPOT", you might use that time to spotlight the talents of the youth, inviting them to compete in sports tournaments, or to perform: singing, dancing, or doing poetic readings. Unchurched youth will be far more attracted when your youth invite them to "the spot" than they would be when invited to church. In this way, you meet their needs and accomplish your outreach goal at the same time.

Begin with just a monthly gathering, then as interest and numbers grow you may decide to host it on a weekly basis. As long as meetings are always held at their regular time and place, area youth will look forward to a gathering filled with excitement and energy. Be sure to allow them to make suggestions about the program planning, and to be involved in the night's activities.

Encourage a competition between your young people, and reward those who bring the greatest number of guests. Remember that responsibility brings about accountability. You cannot blame your youth if the attendance is poor, if you don't give them an incentive to come and bring a guest.

FUN NIGHT: This is a night during the week that becomes known for its food, games and fellowship. It's helpful to have a theme that dictates decorations, the focus of the night, and even what the young people wear to the event. The biggest responsibility youth should have in this event is simply to invite others, to be present and participate. This event allows them to bring their friends to discover what the youth department has to offer. Be prepared to welcome guests and obtain contact information, for follow-up purposes. The leader in charge should be responsible for organizing the food and games for the night. This event can also be used to highlight the accomplishments of participants, for example, giving awards for most faithful attendance at Bible study, or for "most involved youth."

COMMUNITY AWARENESS DAY: This is a day of the week, usually a Saturday, when the youth director, youth leaders, and young people gather to go out into the community to spread the word about, and invite new people, to youth department events. This can be as simple as going to a mall, park or local community center to distribute tracts and/or information packets. Or it can be as complex as choosing a neighborhood block to clean and restore, or visiting a group home to donate necessities they lack. Consider going door to door in your local neighborhood. Often times, those who live near the church, have never had anyone visit, witness or pray for specific needs or invite them to services. Whatever site you choose, remember that your target audience is youth, and your goal is to make the community aware of what you have to offer.

PARK SERVICES: What is more attractive than youth and others praising and magnifying Christ outdoors? This is an unusual and an often welcome sight. It attracts the attention of both believers and unbelievers. Many will be drawn simply by curiosity; however, this is your opportunity to minister, invite, and inform them about your church and youth department. This service often requires collaboration with other departments in your church but be sure to have a representative, preferably a young person, share what's going on in your youth department. This will inspire spectators to come and be part of the action.

OPEN FORUMS: It is important to provide a place for young people to discuss worrisome issues and ask questions about how to handle challenges they face on a daily basis. Often times, young people have questions that are not addressed in Bible study sessions or even during youth worship services. You should allow time for question and answers during Bible study, but who wants to risk embarrassment if they ask an intimate question in an atmosphere that doesn't protect their privacy? The solution: host a monthly open forum where young people are invited to anonymously submit questions and ideas for discussion. Announce that questions must be submitted one week before the forum, so that leaders have time to pray and brainstorm the scriptural way of wisdom on tough subjects. You might even consider inviting an expert or panel guest to answer questions regarding a particular topic in which the youth express high interest. How do you attract youth to an open forum? Guarantee that their questions will be addressed in a respectful way, while protecting their anonymity. If the questions are of interest and they are able to trust the leadership, they will not miss the session, and may even invite their friends to join them. It's important to realize that they have probably discussed the same subjects with their peers. Now you have the incredible honor of offering wise counsel through a guided discussion.

JUVENILE HALL OUTREACH – "Behind Closed Doors":

This project is generally spearheaded by the adults working in the youth ministry. This is only due to the limitations and restrictions of most Juvenile Detention Centers. We must not forget about the sons and daughters that have erred in the past, but are searching for a better way to live. Many of the children who are in juvenile hall are from your local area. However, just because you failed to reach them before their mistake, don't assume it's too late. Organize your staff and write up an agenda that will work for "at-risk and troubled youth" of all ages. Be aware that children as young as seven and eight years old are housed in some Juvenile Detention Centers. Your message should focus on hope. Be ready to offer them information and directions to your church or provide a list of other local churches they may want to attend upon their release. For the most part, these youth need only hear that they are and can be somebody important, someone God will use to impact the world around them. However, they also require intense follow-up and ongoing positive reinforcement. Partner with the Juvenile Detention Center chaplain and create a strategy that allows you to contact the youth upon their release. Although your youth may not directly participate in this outreach, allow them to make suggestions regarding your presentation.

These projects will be more effective if you have an identifier that indicates who you are and where you're from. For example: t-shirts, hats, etc. Not only does it serve this purpose, but it demonstrates **unity!** Do not forget to fast and pray for wisdom and direction before going out to win the lost. *(...men ought always to pray, and not to faint – Luke 18:1).*

Youth Leaders' Discussion Forum

1. Define evangelism the way you think a young person would define it.

2. Why do you think it's important for evangelism to occur internally, before reaching out? How do you interpret the phrase "in-reach comes before outreach"?

3. After considering the outreach projects previously listed, which project is more appealing to you? Why? Offer other recommendations for outreach projects that are not listed.

Chapter 3

EDUCATIONAL DEVELOPMENT

Study to shew thyself approved unto God, a workman that needeth not to be ashamed rightly dividing the word of truth (II Timothy 2:15).

What is education and why is it important?

Education is the act of training and or schooling an individual regarding a particular subject. It oversees the mental and moral growth of an individual.

It's imperative that we offer education that addresses the physical, emotional and spiritual needs of young people. Education serves as the foundation for purpose. If we fail to meet those needs they will never live up to their potential or live out their divine destiny. A person's purpose reveals itself as we nurture his or her innate gifting and talents. Wise instruction enables us to nurture the unknown potential that reveals itself in due time.

It's not enough to tell our youth that they have the potential to become lawyers, doctors or gifted speakers. We must offer resources within our youth departments that will prepare them to become what and who they want to be. It's important to speak life to them, emphasizing that they can do all things through Christ. If they are consistently told that they are destined for greatness, they will eventually believe and seek wisdom regarding the route to such success. However, if they are told that they are nothing and have nothing to offer, they will believe they have nothing of value that God can use, and little reason to live. Remember that **death and life are in the power of the tongue... (Proverbs 18:21).** Guard your lips from speaking death words, because it will nullify the good fruit you want to produce.

How do I educate youth naturally?

Unless your ministry has chartered an accredited educational program, your youth will obtain most of their knowledge from public and private schools. Your role is simply to reinforce or add to what they have learned. There are a number of methods you can use to reinforce and emphasize the importance of education. You must first demonstrate that education is important to you. Youth need to observe that you have a sincere interest in education. That doesn't imply that you must acquire a Master's Degree or Ph.D. It simply means that you deliberately challenge youth to broaden their horizons, making it a habit to read and study.

Below I've listed a few suggestions that can enhance the educational component of your youth department. These options can be combined and or modified to meet the educational demands of your young people.

- Tutoring Programs
- Professional Presentations
- How-to-Clinics
- College Mentoring Programs

TUTORING PROGRAMS: Choose a particular day(s) of the week and use it to regularly help young people with their studies. Ensure that tutors have the skills necessary to address the basic needs of the students. For example, an adult whose expertise is history may not be effective in tutoring a young person who struggles with math. Identify individuals within your church who are blessed with the aptitude to teach basic subjects. For example, Math, English, Economics, etc. This project can also serve as a calling for gifted young people who are willing to tutor others. Spread the word far and wide that on a specific day and time, young people of all ages can come and get help with their homework. Can you see the potential harvest from such an outreach? When we welcome everyone and offer to promote their success we also have an opportunity to invite them to visit the youth ministry with the same encouraging theme. As your department and youth staff flourish, consider offering tutoring services more than once a week.

This particular project does not require volunteers to wear the formal title of "youth leader." However, the youth leader of this project must be energetic and organized. Those who volunteer to help only need to have a passion for the subject they are tutoring and patience to work with young people. The requirements for tutors are simply **passion** and **patience.**

PROFESSIONAL PRESENTATIONS: This project requires that you search out the professional interests of your youth. Discover which of your young people wants to be a lawyer, doctor, dentist, etc. Then contact professionals who would be willing to give a presentation to those with such interests.

Ideally, this event will be held once a month. Advertise, announcing the date of the presentation, the topic of discussion and the name of the speaker. This project will require extensive planning by the coordinator, who is responsible to identify the interests of the youth, enlist the aid of an expert speaker, and create an environment for learning. Presentations of this nature provide information and inspire youth to pursue their fields of interest.

HOW-TO-CLINICS: These are sessions, usually lasting one or two hours, that focus on a teaching youth a particularly appealing skill. For example: how to write an essay, how to give presentations, how to study for a test, etc. These clinics should be conducted by individuals who have expertise on the subject. To be effective, you should host a clinic a minimum of once a month. Again, inform your community and local school leaders that this service is available through your ministry.

COLLEGE MENTORING PROGRAMS: Contact the local directors of college career centers and campus affairs. Your goal is to identify students whose academic performance is above average and who are involved in student activities. Be very cautious when selecting an "unknown" person to be a mentor for your youth. Consult your pastor regarding the selection process. Once you have chosen those you want to enlist, let them know what you expect and make sure you're on the same page. Whether you expect them to tutor or be presenters at how-to sessions, they should have the ability of establishing easy rapport with the families of those they mentor. If all goes well, students may become close enough to attend graduation or award ceremonies for their mentors, giving them an inside track to observe the rewards that come from making the effort to learn, so they too are motivated to strive for excellence.

In your quest to find mentors, it can help if you partner with nearby colleges and/or their well-established fraternities or sororities. Such organizations usually have mentoring programs your youth department may be able to use to your advantage.

How can I make certain that the youth are spiritually equipped for life?

Simply organize a powerful Bible study hour. Below are two suggestions that will help ignite a passion for studying the Word and loving God and others.

- Youth Bible Study - YBS
- Bible Institute

YOUTH BIBLE STUDY: Again, you don't have to refer to a Bible study by that name. You can label your Bible study as, "The Word Session", "W.W.W. – Wednesday Word and Worship." Be creative! You can use commercially-prepared resources or create your own, as long as they're true to the Word. Keep in mind that props and visual aids demonstrate your lesson far better than mere words, and give your students a visible example to hold onto. Instructors should always come well prepared, becoming familiar with the subject before a class session. If the presenter is ill prepared, students will instantly sense it, and lose interest. Why should they listen if teachers aren't interested enough to prepare? Your youth should have a copy, whether hard or electronic, of the lesson you are teaching. You want them to have something to take home and share with others. Give awards to those who actively participate and faithfully attend Bible study. Youth usually need frequent positive reinforcement to prevent them from becoming bored. It's up to you to create a fun, energetic learning atmosphere, so they delight in coming instead of losing interest.

BIBLE INSTITUTE: This is usually a six-week Bible study program that is normally held on the same night each week or in lieu of a regular Bible study. Unlike the variety afforded in a weekly Bible study, the Bible institute focuses on a specific book of the Bible and the goal is to go deep enough to master the material therein contained. For example: If you choose to study the book of Acts for a six-week session, understand that you must complete at least four chapters a week in order to complete the book by the end of the session. Encourage youth to read the chapters prior to each session so that they are prepared to discuss them and ask questions. During the Bible institute sessions, the instructor's task is to discuss the main points of each chapter. Challenge your youth and give them written exams before and after your six-week program. This will not only gauge your effectiveness as an instructor, but it will give students a way to measure the success of the learning experience, comparing the before and after test results. At the close of each Bible institute, schedule a graduation ceremony that offers a certificate of completion, as well as recognizing those with faithful attendance. Such recognition increases the excitement and motivation for learning.

What are other methods of promoting education?

1. Scholarship awards/Luncheon
2. Graduation Ceremony
3. Tours of educational institutions

Organize a church dinner or luncheon in recognition of the academic achievements of your youth. This event can also be used as a fundraiser if you sell tickets and use the profit to award scholarships to your deserving students. Though chances are slim that scholarships will pay their semester's tuition, it may help them with books or travel expenses. Finances will limit the number of students who receive a monetary sum, but everyone should receive recognition for their efforts.

Obtain permission from your Pastor to host an annual Graduation Day. This can also be a part of the regular worship service if desired. Use this opportunity to allow youth to wear their graduation regalia including hats, robes and honor cords. This service should include graduates from kindergarten through college (youth and young adults). You should have a preliminary and post procession of the graduates. Glean ideas from a standard graduation ceremony. Select a valedictorian and salutatorian from the list of participants. This will encourage those who may have excelled academically, but received little recognition in the public school setting. A student may have a GPA ranking them 10th in their graduating class, but ranked first to graduate among the youth of your church. Allow both the valedictorian and salutatorian to address the attendees and graduates. Include an inspirational keynote speaker. Be prepared to reward each graduate with a certificate of recognition.

Again, establish a relationship with personnel of college career centers and arrange a tour of each campus. Universities usually welcome a visit of this nature and are apt to make your visit pleasant and informative.

Youth Leaders' Discussion Forum

1. What kind of natural and spiritual impact does education have on students?

2. Identify one educational method that you can immediately implement in your youth department. Why did you choose this method?

3. Besides the methods previously mentioned, identify and discuss other methods of promoting education.

Chapter 4

ACTIVE AUXILIARIES

I must work the works of him that sent me, while it is day... (St. John 9:4).

Why are active auxiliaries vital to a youth department?

Auxiliaries are the foundation, the outlet that allows our youth to discover and express their gifts and talents, showcasing their indispensable value within the group. The operative word here is **active!** It's not enough to have a junior usher board when there are no youth participants. It's imperative that you appoint energetic youth leaders over each youth auxiliary. Youth leaders must ensure that youth are not only excited to be involved, but are disappointed when they are not. Create an atmosphere that embraces the concept of a team or "family." Youth should understand how important they are to each other and to your department.

Auxiliaries allow youth to step out into their God-given ministries and use their talents. Below are suggested auxiliaries that should exist within your youth department.

- Junior Pulpit Aides/Junior Deacons
- Youth Hospitality Workers
- Youth Bible Study
- Youth Prayer Clinics
- Athletics Division
- Encouragement Staff
- Newsletter and Yearbook Staff
- Youth Fellowships/Socials
- Youth Fundraisers
- Drama Team
- Drill Team & Honor Guard
- Sign Language Team
- Praise Dancers
- Youth Praise & Worship Team
- Youth Choir
- Outreach and Missions

Identify a youth leader for each auxiliary and provide them the opportunity to present their vision, purpose and mission for the auxiliary. Their purpose and vision should align with that of the youth director.

Youth leaders should give the youth director an agenda of the days, times and locations of auxiliary meetings that focus either on business or activities. It should also include their annual agenda to be distributed to the youth involved in the auxiliary.

Reports of this nature are to be submitted at least once a year. The youth director should revisit their proposal during the interim of time to see whether youth leaders are making progress toward the goals listed in their proposal. If they aren't making progress the youth director should assist them toward that end.

The youth director should be able to organize a yearly calendar based on the proposals given by each of the auxiliary leaders. This is for organizational purposes in order to avoid calendar conflicts. Keep in mind that your youth will usually be involved in more than one auxiliary. Each auxiliary leader should endeavor to support other auxiliaries as well. Many times, different auxiliaries will participate in the same event. For example, the drama team, praise dancers, youth praise and worship team, junior ushers and pulpit aides, may all play a role in Youth Night Gatherings. Everyone must work together in order to achieve the team goal. As the youth director, you must emphasize the importance of unity. There should be no competition among auxiliaries or their leaders.

Auxiliaries are designed for and cater to the youth. They also attract and inspire them to participate in areas where their gifts are needed. The ultimate result is a growing and thriving youth department.

Description of Auxiliaries:

Junior Pulpit Aides/Junior Deacons: This auxiliary is designed to train youth, both male and female, on how to conduct themselves when assisting with matters of the pulpit. This includes how to serve water, mints, etc. to the pulpit staff. Junior deacons, are usually but are not limited to males. They should also be trained to serve effectively when receiving public offerings and how to assist the elders and ministers of the church.

Youth Hospitality Workers: Establish a team of junior workers and train them to greet and welcome guests, with special emphasis on serving special guests who may visit your church for youth events.

Youth Bible Study: This auxiliary is designed to enhance the natural and spiritual growth and maturity of the youth. Youth Bible study and education programs come under the auspices of this auxiliary, which is also responsible for health and wellness education.

Youth Prayer Clinics: Identify a day and time convenient for the schedules of young people. Remember, they cannot attend 12:00 noon prayer or 6:00 a.m. prayer if it is held on weekdays. Allow youth the opportunity to gather and pray, virtually or physically. Teach them how to pray in faith, expecting God to move. Encourage them to cry out to God and believe for great things. This auxiliary is also responsible for hosting overnight prayer sessions.

Athletics Division: This auxiliary should make available sports of all kinds including basketball, baseball, tennis, etc. Partner with your local community centers or churches if you do not have the appropriate facilities for practices or games. Inquire about the Christian athletic leagues in your area and join them. This will allow your youth to participate in friendly competition and fellowship, while networking with others.

Encouragement Staff: This team of young people is responsible for uplifting the spirits of others. This can be as simple as sending a card to let them know someone is thinking of them or praying for them. This team should also form a birthday club and be responsible for recognizing special events in the lives of young people. Again, this can be as simple as a birthday card or a mention in the youth newsletter.

Newsletter and Yearbook Staff: Establish a team of young people who are gifted in writing, photography and information systems. Publish a monthly or quarterly newsletter that captures highlights of past and upcoming events, and include noteworthy youth accomplishments. For example: highlight the special efforts of the youth during that particular quarter, mention honor roll students, or those who may have excelled athletically at their school. At the close of each year, a yearbook that records such highlights should be made available. This can be a fundraiser; however, it is also a memoir that youth will cherish. This auxiliary may also be responsible for creating and maintaining a department website or social media presence.

Youth Fellowships/Socials: This auxiliary is responsible for organizing field trips and local area youth fellowship gatherings. This can include a trip to Six Flags, museums, or hosting a talent hour at your local church. Encourage the members of this auxiliary to invite youth from other churches as well as youth in your community.

Youth Fundraisers: This auxiliary plays a major role in your youth department, organizing events to raise the funds that sponsor youth activities. This team can partner with the youth fellowship/social auxiliary in order to host events that include both fellowship and fundraising. Challenge your youth to plan fundraisers outside of dinner sales and bake sales. Your goal is to sponsor fundraisers that will earn substantial amounts so that your staff members do not become "burned out" with fundraising events. Don't forget to aggressively pursue grant funding if you have a non-profit status.

Drama Team: This auxiliary serves as an outlet that allows youth to minister and communicate through acting. They are responsible for presenting dramatizations, plays, and skits during special occasions such as Resurrection Sunday and Christmas. Encourage them to also organize events in the off season. These plays, skits or dramatizations should have a theme and target to reach, conveying a specific message to youth.

Drill Team & Honor Guard: Drill teams and honor guard members minister through choreographed, synchronized stepping and scriptural shouts. Drill teams usually perform much like college fraternities and sororities, while the performance of the honor guard tends to use a military style.

Sign Language Team: Be prepared to minister to the whole person. You may have young people within your department who are hearing-impaired or deaf or who just want to learn sign language. Members of this team use sign language to convey a spoken or written word, idea, wish or command. Select a song and sign the words of the song. This presentation should also have a theme.

Praise Dancers: This auxiliary is made up of young people who express their admiration to God by moving rhythmically to music and using gestures and steps that convey a particular message. Again, the movements should concur and be in sync with the words of the songs.

Youth Praise & Worship Team: Establish a group a young people who are responsible for conducting praise and worship during youth services. This group should know how important their role is to the worship experience. It's their responsibility to usher in the Spirit of God through singing and exultations. Their sincere, passionate worship sets the tone for your service, ushering others into His presence.

Youth Choir: Give those who are not able to sing on the praise and worship team the opportunity to sing as part of the youth choir. Most youth are bashful when it comes to singing alone or small groups, but are apt to sing with others in a larger group setting. The choir should practice at least once a week and be prepared to minister in song at the request of the youth director.

Outreach and Missions: Establish a group of young people who enjoy ministering and assisting those who are less fortunate. Organize projects such as food basket donations, clothing drives, and visits to convalescent homes. Allow them to experience the joy of giving to others knowing that it is more blessed to give than to receive *(Acts 20:35)*.

Lawanne' S. Grant

Youth Leaders' Discussion Forum

1. What would your youth department look like without active auxiliaries?

2. Considering the present state of your youth department, identify and discuss 3 auxiliaries that you could activate immediately.

3. Considering where you want your youth department to be in 6 months, name 3 auxiliaries that you can work toward implementing.

Chapter 5

ANNUAL AFFAIRS

Not forsaking the assembling of ourselves together, as the manner of some is, but exhorting one another: and so much more, as ye see the day approaching (Hebrews 10:25).

What type of annual affairs should my youth department host?

As youth directors, you should host annual events that hold the attention of young people and keep them motivated and involved between eagerly-anticipated major events. Each year these events should grow and participation should increase. Annual affairs allow young people to anticipate them with great excitement. You must give them something about which to get excited or they may lose interest and drop out.

Below are a few suggestions that you may want to consider for annual affairs:

- King and Queen Pageant

- Annual Youth Conference
- Winter Ball
- Scholarship Banquet
- Youth Retreat
- Annual Cookout

KING and QUEEN PAGEANT: Host an annual pageant to crown a male as Mr. _____ (name of your ministry) and a female as Ms. _____, (name of your ministry) and use this as a major fundraiser. Assign the youth to collect funds from sponsors of their choice, then reward them for the funds they collect. For example, every $50 donation is worth 10 bonus points. These points should be added to the final score earned during the actual pageant. The primary requisite is that pageant participants be actively involved in youth department activities. There are generally three segments of a pageant; (1) Introduction, (2) Talent, and (3) Questions and Answers. You should come up with a fair and unbiased process to judge participants regarding presentation, speech, creativity, etc. You should also choose individuals outside of your immediate church to judge the pageant, just to avoid the appearance of conflict of interest. The selected King and Queen are charged with the duty of promoting, representing, and working in tandem with leaders of the youth department during their year-long reign.

ANNUAL YOUTH CONFERENCE: Schedule a few dates in a particular month and host a youth conference at the same time every year. Be as consistent as possible in your planning. Youth conferences differ slightly from youth weekends and youth extravaganzas. This is a weekend that is comprised of powerful preaching and teaching usually delivered by a special guest speaker. An outline of conference classes should also be made available, in order to stir up interest in advance. This project can be a fundraiser for your youth department. After analyzing the conference budget, set an affordable registration fee, and offer the information to your church and the surrounding area. Make your conference available to everyone. A youth conference is usually a three or four-day affair. Below is a standard itinerary for a youth conference. You should add or delete agenda items to accommodate your specific goals, and include ideas from your youth and youth leaders.

- **Thursday** @ 7:00pm: Conference choir rehearsal (consider adding a special musical guest)

- **Friday Night** @ 7:30pm: Opening Worship Service – Guest Speaker

- **Saturday Morning** @ 9:00am – 12:00pm: Youth Conference classes 12:00pm – 1:00pm: Youth Luncheon

- **Saturday Night** @7:00pm: Youth Musical featuring Conference Choir and special musical guest

- **Sunday Morning** @ 8:00am: Youth Prayer Breakfast

- **Sunday Morning** @ 11:00am: Worship Service – Guest Speaker

- **Sunday Night** @ 7:00pm: Final Worship Service – Guest Speaker

Create a theme for your conference based on a scripture. Your conference agenda including speaker's messages, classes and activities should be centered around that theme. Be intentional about showcasing your active auxiliaries during the conference.

WINTER BALL: Again, this event can be a fundraiser for your department. It's generally scheduled for the month of December, and can be held at your church facility, community center, or local hotel ballroom. Establish a profitable but reasonable price for your tickets. Youth should dress formally for this event. Make arrangements for professional photographers to be available. This is a night where your youth can invite their school friends and family members. You should establish a theme for your ball, and your program should reflect that theme. Be sure to connect with your local bridal and tuxedo shops to determine if they would be willing to waive or discount rental fees and allow the youth to model (advertise) their attire at the special event.

SCHOLARSHIP BANQUET: This event is usually held during the month of June immediately after public school graduations and prior to the departure of youth leaving for college. Annual scholarships should be given to graduating seniors who are attending institutions in order to further their education. Use ticket sales to finance scholarships. Invite local school dignitaries, elected officials, community leaders, and business owners. Your program should include, but not be limited to, achievements of the scholarship recipients and an

Lawanne' S. Grant

inspirational speaker.

YOUTH RETREAT: Youth retreats allow time to refocus and gain insight. It provides youth leaders an opportunity to embrace newcomers and encourage those already involved. It also allows the youth director to share his/her goals for the year with youth and youth leaders. Identify a camp site and plan a camping trip with your youth. Ideally, you should plan this trip at the beginning of each year but it's also fine to organize it during the summer. Your agenda should include interactive games and activities that enhance the spiritual growth of the young people. This includes everything from scavenger hunts to morning prayer, held around the campfire or another designated area. It's important to be creative and to have a full agenda planned for your young people, so that they are occupied and engaged at all times during the event.

ANNUAL COOKOUT: Schedule a day in the summer months when your youth host an annual youth cookout. Be prepared to play volleyball, softball, water games, etc. This is simply designed for young people to invite others and to enjoy fellowship with one another. Allow youth to spearhead the project, including cooking and organizing the activities.

These are exciting events that will keep your youth inspired and engaged. At this age, they often tend to shy away from church because they feel of little value there. If they are involved, they are apt to feel they are making a valuable contribution. As a result, they grow, blossom, and walk into their divine destiny. As youth directors and leaders, it's your task to keep them on a straight and narrow path until they are able to wisely decipher those things that are and are not edifying to their spirits.

Lawanne' S. Grant

Youth Leaders' Discussion Forum

1. Does your youth department currently sponsor an annual event? Discuss what you are doing well and identify areas that need improvement.

2. What annual youth affairs have other churches sponsored that you would like to implement in your church? Speak to the way that event would fit into the paradigm of your ministry.

3. Select one of the suggested annual affairs. Consult your young people for input and use their suggestions as a starting point. Discuss the steps you will take to offer this annual affair to your youth department.

Chapter 6

WRITE IT &
MAKE IT HAPPEN

Now that you know more about the five-point thrust, let's apply each principle to your youth department. The following will help you develop foundational principles and write a projected one-year event calendar. Consider this your strategic plan, and consult it often to ensure that your youth are thriving, headed in the right direction. Are you ready? Let's write it and make it happen!

The vision for my youth department is:

_____

_____

_____

_____

_____

_____

Lawanne' S. Grant

The individual(s) who will work closely with me to fulfill this vision is:

_____

_____

I will obtain permission to utilize the following people because they demonstrate the ability to passionately lead youth.

Youth Leader   Auxiliary of Interest

1._____

2._____

3._____

4._____

5._____

6._____

7._____

8._____

9._____

10._____

I will ask for a detailed proposal from the youth leaders no later than (date)_____. The proposal should identify the plan of action for the auxiliary, with the help of assistant staff members and junior staff members.

My youth department will host a Youth Night Gathering every _____ of the month. The name of the gathering will be _____.

I will reward the youth who brings the greatest number of guests to the gathering with _____.

My youth department will host a Fun Night once every _____.

The youth and youth leaders will go out to witness every _____ of the month starting at _____a.m. until _____p.m.

We will partner with _____ to create community awareness of our ministry every _____.

My youth department will host at least one park service during the month of _____.

Lawanne' S. Grant

We will host opens forums every _____ of the month. I believe the right leader to spearhead this project is _____.

I will contact the director of my local Juvenile Detention Center no later than _____. We will visit and minister to the youth at Juvenile Hall at least _____ times a year.

I will make available identifiers (t-shirts, hats, etc.) for those in my youth department no later than _____.

I will implement a tutoring program by _____ and will alert other churches and schools of this service.

We will host professional presentations and How-to-Clinics every _____ weekend of the month.

I will contact Student Affairs of _____ University to determine if they are available to assist with tutoring and or mentoring programs.

Youth Bible study will convene weekly on _____ at _____p.m. (day of week)

Our Bible institute will be a _____-week session and will begin _____.

We will host a scholarship luncheon in order to raise funds during the month of _____.

Our graduation ceremony will be held in the month of _____ before college-bound students depart for school.

I will take my youth to visit the University of _____ during the month of _____, but before the end of this year.

The auxiliaries that I hope are fully operational by the end of the year include:

1._____

2._____

3._____

4._____

5._____

6._____

7._____

8._____

9._____

10._____

These auxiliaries will meet every _____.

The two major affairs that our youth department will host this year are:

1._____

2._____

I will revisit this plan of action on _____.

Youth Leaders' Discussion Forum

1. Identify immediate resources available to you and your team that can assist with fulfilling the stated vision.

2. What are potential barriers to executing this plan of action? How will you overcome them?

3. Discuss how you will celebrate hallmarks of success with your youth and youth leaders.

Chapter 7

CONCLUSION

Let the information offered herein serve as the foundation for effective youth ministry. Jesus told Peter that upon this rock (Petro –a little rock) I will build my church and the gates of hell shall not prevail against it (Matthew 16:13-18).

It is imperative that you have spiritual focus, direction, and vision for your youth department. As youth directors and youth leaders, you should remain prayerful always seeking knowledge, wisdom, and guidance from God. Remember that young people are a unique group of individuals who require powerful and anointed leaders.

The following is a list of recommendations to keep in mind when organizing, establishing, and conducting activities within your youth department.

- Allow young people to occupy major roles within your youth department.

- Openly reward and acknowledge the diligent work of youth and youth leaders. Always accentuate the positive, using every opportunity to express appreciation.

- Be prepared to refer at-risk youth to appropriate agencies, if you are unable to help them.

- Be knowledgeable regarding community programs that assist youth with specific needs.

- Partner with community organizations such as schools, community centers, treatment programs, etc.

- Research and learn how to obtain government funding that is available to faith-based organizations.

- Fellowship with local youth departments of other churches.

- Always provide young people the opportunity to offer input and make suggestions.

- Remain persistent in all your endeavors; never give up, because your answers are right around the corner

- Be sensitive and expect to encounter youth from various backgrounds.

- Make sure your leaders are consistently energetic and passionate.

- Maintain a thriving outreach program.

- Stress the importance of education and goal setting for the future.

- Ensure that your auxiliaries are active, moving in sync with organizational goals.

- Host annual events that involve and welcome youth from various locations.

- Hold fundraisers that produce profitable and substantial sums of money to avoid fundraising burnout.

- Be sure to have a platform for communicating and hearing the voice of the **parents!**

My prayer is not that you have been inspired, for inspiration is merely a temporary burst of excitement. My hope is that this information will empower you to effectively minister to the needs of young people. As leaders, you must stay focused so that no matter what kind of hindrances arise you can be confident of this very thing, that He which hath begun a good work in you, will perform it until the day of Jesus Christ *(Philippians 1:6).*

Stand firm on the foundational principles offered in the 5-point thrust and expect growth as a result of effective youth ministry.

Energetic Leaders ~ Evangelism ~

Educational Development ~

Active Auxiliaries ~ Annual Affairs

Youth Leaders' Discussion Forum

1. What's your biggest take away from what you've read?

2. How has the 5-point thrust shaped your approach to building a firm foundation for your youth ministry?

3. What related topics would you like to be addressed in the future?

I would love to hear your
feedback to these final questions.

Email me: lgrant@leadershipdevelopme.com

Visit our website to discover leadership
development tools available to you:
www.leadershipdevelopme.com